I AM RESTORED

HOW I LOST MY RELIGION
BUT FOUND MY FAITH

STUDY GUIDE | FOUR SESSIONS

LECRAE

With Beth Graybill

Harper*Christian*
Resources

Contents

Introduction

Welcome to the I Am Restored small-group study. This study guide is meant to be a companion to my book I Am Restored. Here's why this study is so important. Throughout my journey to restoration, I've learned the simple truth that we can face our past willingly, or our lives will force us to face it. This choice is not always easy, but it is often painfully clear. We can drown in our dysfunction, or we can choose to go down into what often feels like the valley of the shadow of death—filled with our shame and trauma—to search for hope and healing.

This is where we find restoration. But digging into the deep corners of our souls and excavating our past is the uncomfortable part of the process. It often involves dealing with our own "stuff" from our family of origin so that we are able to find healing and stop duplicating the same patterns—in our rituals or in the ways we raise our kids.

I thought I could find my own restoration by the strength of my own sheer will. But I couldn't outrun the wounds of my past. And as a result, I couldn't ignore the brokenness I experienced. Truth is, I'm still broken. I'm still trying to unpack the effects of my abuse and my father wounds to this day. I've worked hard to purge bitterness and hatred from my heart, but ignoring what was robbed from me isn't easy.

Recovering from my father's absence has been a lifelong process—a painful but necessary engagement with a dark time in my life. Add to that the trauma of abuse, and the trauma of a black kid growing up under systemic racism and violence, and the weight of the dysfunction of my world made me want to run. I was afraid that if I faced the turmoil and the chaos of my past, it would consume me. And I had too much to risk in the present for that: *my music, my family, my fame, my faith, my wife*, and *my life*. So I found ways to numb myself from the pain. And in doing so, I came dangerously close to sabotaging the beautiful family and the wonderful life God gave me. That is, until I found hope and healing.

As Christians, we have a lot of growing to do when it comes to talking about healthy ways to handle trauma and turmoil. In all my years of learning about theology, the church, and the Bible, I hadn't heard anything about trauma or its effect on the human body, even though countless biblical characters clearly struggled with melancholy or depression. Even Jesus wrestled with inner turmoil and pain that drove him to his knees in prayer. But I believe this growth is possible when we start to recognize the gifts God has given some of our brothers and sisters who work as trained counselors and therapists in our communities. When chaotic things happen, we need a narrative to helps us make sense of things so that we can put them into context. This is what therapy does for us . . . and this is how we find healing.

Know this: God is making a masterpiece out of our mess. My brokenness made me stronger than before. The fire of it all forged something new in me. This is the hope of Christ who makes all things new in Jesus. And this is my hope for you—that through this study you will come to know the presence of God, the hope of Jesus, and that you begin to take steps toward healing as well. May you be able to say, "I *am restored.*"

—Lecrae

How to Use This Guide

The I Am Restored video study is designed to be experienced in a group setting (such as a Bible study, Sunday school class, or small-group gathering) and also as an individual study. Each session begins with a welcome section, two questions to get you thinking about the topic, and a reading from the Bible. You will then watch a video with Lecrae, which can be accessed via the streaming code found on the inside front cover. If you are doing the study with a group, you will then engage in some directed discussion. You will close each session with a time of personal reflection and prayer.

Each person in the group should have his or her own copy of this study guide and a Bible. You are also encouraged to have a copy of the I Am Restored book, as reading the book alongside the curriculum will provide you with deeper insights and make the journey more meaningful. See the "For Next Week" section at the end of each between-studies section for the chapter in the book that corresponds to the material your group is discussing.

To get the most out of your group experience, keep the following points in mind. First, the real growth in this study will happen during your small-group time. This is where you will process the video content for the week, ask questions, and learn from others as you hear what God is doing in their lives. For this reason, it is important for you to be fully committed to the group and attend each session so you can build trust and rapport with the other members. If you choose to only go through the motions, or if you refrain from participating, there is a lesser chance you will find what you're looking for during this study.

Second, remember the goal of your small group is to serve as a place where people can share, learn about God, and build intimacy and friendship. For this reason, seek to make your group a safe place. This means being honest about your thoughts and feelings and listening carefully to everyone else's opinion. (If you are a group leader, there are additional instructions and resources in the back of the guide for leading a productive discussion group.)

Third, resist the temptation to fix a problem someone might be having or to correct his or her theology, as that's not the purpose of your small-group time. Also, keep everything your group shares confidential. This will foster a rewarding sense of community in your group and create a place where people can heal, be challenged, and grow spiritually.

Following your group time, reflect on the material you've covered by engaging in the between-session activities. For each session, you may wish to complete the personal study all in one sitting or spread it out over a few days (for example, working on it a half-hour a day on different days that week). Note that if you are unable to finish (or even start!) your between-sessions personal study, you should still attend the group study video session. You are still wanted and welcome to the group even if you don't have your "homework" done.

Keep in mind the videos, discussion questions, and activities are simply meant to kick-start your thoughts so you are open to both what God wants you to hear and how he wants to apply it to your life. As you go through this study, listen to what God is saying to you as you consider your own journey in light of Lecrae's journey of losing his religion and finding his faith as told in I Am Restored.

Facing the Turmoil

In my distress, I called to the LORD;
I called out to my God.

2 SAMUEL 22:7

Welcome

A few years ago, at the height of my career and peak of my influence, I realized my life was in disarray. At first, I just felt "off," but then I had a few episodes of problematic behavior that quickly sank into a spiral of anguish. Maybe I was fooling people on the outside, but on the inside my life was a wreck. I was a sickly mashup of addiction and self-medication.

Looking back, I can see signs that something was happening. But I wasn't willing to face it at the time. I was on tour with a bunch of other artists and teachers I admired. And I had just written about most of my story in my bestselling book *Unashamed*. I seemed to be at the pinnacle of my life and career, and yet on the inside, deep turmoil was brewing in my soul—a restlessness that's hard to describe.

I pushed it away . . . for weeks, then months, and then years. But something was happening that I could no longer ignore. Underneath my problematic behavior, an uncomfortable shift was taking place in my life that threatened to derail all the greatness I had achieved. All the awards and accolades could no longer hide the weakness of my heart. I was broken and had lost sight of myself.

It's easy to say that part of the difficulty of being a public figure is people not recognizing your humanity. But the truth is, the most dangerous part of being a public figure for me was not recognizing my *own* humanity. Regardless of my popularity and professional status, when the lights went off, I was forced to live with myself.

In the middle of all this pain, I realized I didn't have the right "Christian" response. Meaning, I had to dig deeper than just saying I had "struggles" and "trials," as Christians like to call them. I had to acknowledge that I was actually dealing with *trauma* . . . and this trauma required me to address deep root issues from my past.

I was challenged by specialists and friends to interrogate my past and take an honest look at dark places I thought I had overcome. If I truly wanted to heal, I *had* to face the turmoil in my life. And I'm here to tell you, if I can do it, you can too. I am living proof that there is hope and healing on the other side of the chaos and pain if you're willing to face the turmoil.

Share

If you or any of your group members are just getting to know one another, take a few minutes to introduce yourselves. Then, to kick things off, briefly discuss one of the following questions:

- What is one hope or expectation you have for this study?

  —o r—

- What are some of the common ways you see people dealing with turmoil and emotional distress?

Read

Invite someone to read aloud Genesis 32:9–32. Listen for fresh insights as you hear the verses being read, and then discuss the questions that follow.

⁹ Then Jacob prayed, "O God of my father Abraham, God of my father Isaac, Lord, you who said to me, 'Go back to your country and your relatives, and I will make you prosper,' ¹⁰ I am unworthy of all the kindness and faithfulness you have shown your servant. I had only my staff when I crossed this Jordan, but now I have become two camps. ¹¹ Save me, I pray, from the hand of my brother Esau, for I am afraid he will come and attack me, and also the mothers with their children. ¹² But you have said, 'I will surely make you prosper and will make your descendants like the sand of the sea, which cannot be counted.'"

¹³ He spent the night there, and from what he had with him he selected a gift for his brother Esau: ¹⁴ two hundred female goats and twenty male goats, two hundred ewes and twenty rams, ¹⁵ thirty female camels with their young, forty cows and ten bulls, and twenty female donkeys and ten male donkeys. ¹⁶ He put them in the care of his servants, each herd

by itself, and said to his servants, "Go ahead of me, and keep some space between the herds."

¹⁷ He instructed the one in the lead: "When my brother Esau meets you and asks, 'Who do you belong to, and where are you going, and who owns all these animals in front of you?' ¹⁸ then you are to say, 'They belong to your servant Jacob. They are a gift sent to my lord Esau, and he is coming behind us.'"

¹⁹ He also instructed the second, the third and all the others who followed the herds: "You are to say the same thing to Esau when you meet him. ²⁰ And be sure to say, 'Your servant Jacob is coming behind us.'" For he thought, "I will pacify him with these gifts I am sending on ahead; later, when I see him, perhaps he will receive me." ²¹ So Jacob's gifts went on ahead of him, but he himself spent the night in the camp.

²² That night Jacob got up and took his two wives, his two female servants and his eleven sons and crossed the ford of the Jabbok. ²³ After he had sent them across the stream, he sent over all his possessions. ²⁴ So Jacob was left alone, and a man wrestled with him till daybreak. ²⁵ When the man saw that he could not overpower him, he touched the socket of Jacob's hip so that his hip was wrenched as he wrestled with the man. ²⁶ Then the man said, "Let me go, for it is daybreak."

But Jacob replied, "I will not let you go unless you bless me."

²⁷ The man asked him, "What is your name?"

"Jacob," he answered.

²⁸ Then the man said, "Your name will no longer be Jacob, but Israel, because you have struggled with God and with humans and have overcome."

²⁹ Jacob said, "Please tell me your name."

But he replied, "Why do you ask my name?" Then he blessed him there.

³⁰ So Jacob called the place Peniel, saying, "It is because I saw God face to face, and yet my life was spared."

³¹ The sun rose above him as he passed Peniel, and he was limping because of his hip. ³² Therefore to this day the Israelites do not eat the tendon attached to the socket of the hip, because the socket of Jacob's hip was touched near the tendon.

Why was Jacob in great fear and distress? What is significant about his wrestling with God?

What kind of distress is causing you to wrestle with God right now?

The Context

Jacob was the son of Isaac and Rebekah, brother to Esau, and husband to Rachel and Leah. Before Jacob became the founding father of the nation of Israel, he was an opportunist, a liar, and a conspirator. He was negligent and untrustworthy at times and was a husband and father who picked favorites. In other words, Jacob was just like us. He had a past full of shame, failure, and regret. He needed to confront the issues of his past so he could move forward with God. This passage represents the turning point in his life: the moment he had to stop running and come face to face with God.

Watch

Play the video segment for session one (see the streaming video access provided on the inside front cover). As you watch, use the following outline to record any thoughts or concepts that stand out to you.

Facing the past in the present

The realization that the past affects the present

Facing the pain of childhood abuse and trauma

Telling your story as a first step to restoration

Emotional wounds must be addressed to be healed

God's presence can bring health, healing, and restoration

God promises to never leave us or forsake us

But this doesn't mean we will all be instantly healthy

Unhealthy attitudes we can bring into our relationship with God

The shift: starting to see the chaos

The brokenness of Christians heralded as a picture of health

The different perspectives in the church and society on race

How we as Christians tend to face pain

We minimize it

We over-spiritualize it

We memorialize it

Look at your story . . . and admit where you need God's healing

Character Study

In the Gospel of John, we read the story of Peter's denial. In chapter 13, the disciples are celebrating the Passover Feast in the upper room of a house. Jesus has just finished washing the feet of the disciples and is talking about some kind of betrayal. In fact, he dismisses Judas on the spot to "do quickly" what he was about to do—betray Christ. Then Jesus starts talking about leaving sometime soon, and he gives the disciples a command to love one another as Jesus has loved them. Confused and surprised, Peter asks Jesus where he's going and if he can follow Jesus. He confesses that he would lay down his life for Jesus. But Jesus answers Peter, "Will you really lay down your life for me? Very truly I tell you, before the rooster crows, you will disown me three times!" (verse 38).

In John 18, the scene is set for Peter to deny Christ. Jesus has been arrested and is being questioned by the high priest. Peter is in the crowd watching. He hangs around outside the courtyard where Jesus is being questioned. He is identified not once, not twice, but three times as one of the disciples of Jesus. Peter denies the acknowledgment every single time.

It's easy to point a finger at Peter and accuse him of treason. But what would you do? In fact, what *do* you do when your life is "on the line"?

Peter knew the weight of denial—the shame, the regret, the failure of betraying one of his best friends, a man he looked up to and loved. And yet his story didn't end there. After Jesus's resurrection, he and the disciples gathered around a fire for a meal. Jesus asked Peter, "Simon son of John, do you love me more than these?" Peter replied, "Yes, Lord. You know that I love you" (John 21:15). Peter and Jesus went back and forth in conversation. Jesus said to Peter, "Feed my lambs . . . take care of my sheep . . . follow me!" (verses 15, 17, 19).

In other words, Jesus not only forgave Peter but also gave him something purposeful to do for the kingdom of God. And that's what Jesus wants to do with you . . . if you're willing to face your denial.

Discuss

Take a few minutes with your group members to discuss what you just watched and explore these concepts in Scripture.

1. What stood out to you from listening to Lecrae today? How has the turmoil or chaos in your life shaped your own story?

2. Lecrae noted that the first step in his journey toward restoration was to admit that the wounds of his past were affecting his present reality. Why do you think we often overlook this truth that our past wounds have an impact on us today?

3. Read 2 Samuel 12:7–14. In this scene, David is confronted by the prophet Nathan to come to terms with a sin he committed in the past. Why do you think the Lord chose to expose David's sin in this way? What does this say about the process that God will often take us through to bring our past to light so we can move forward?

4. Lecrae mentions three unhealthy ways that Christians tend to deal with pain: *minimize* it, *over-spiritualize* it, or *memorialize* it. When have you been guilty using one of these strategies to cope with your pain? What is the best way to deal with pain from your past?

5. Lecrae discussed the rejection he felt from God's people when he began to confront the chaos in his past and in his present and how this led to him "lumping them in" with God. He felt that God had turned his back on him—because that is what God's people had done. Yet the reality is that God has promised to "be with you wherever you go" (Joshua 1:9). How does this promise stand in spite of how other Christians may be treating you?

6. Lecrae notes that sometimes we move too fast, when we would be better served to slow down and look through our story. As you look back, how has God turned your suffering into hope and healing? Where do you need more of God's healing in your life?

Respond

Briefly review the outline for the video teaching and any notes you took. In the space below, write down the most significant point you took away from this session.

Pray

Pray as a group before you close your time together. Ask God to open your hearts and minds and allow you to see the places in your own life and deep in your own heart where you're experiencing turmoil and chaos. Ask God for the hope and healing that only he can provide.

Between-Sessions Personal Study

Reflect on the material you have covered during this week's group time by engaging in the following personal studies. Each day offers a short reading adapted from I Am *Restored*, along with a few reflection questions to take you deeper into the theme of this week's study. (You may also want to review chapters 1–2 in the book before you begin.) Be sure to read the reflection questions and make a few notes in your guide about the experience. At the start of your next group session, you will have a few minutes to share any insights that you learned.

Day 1: Wounded and Broken

Read: Luke 22:7–30; Isaiah 53:1–12; 1 Peter 2:21–25

I was never tough enough for any of the men in my life. And my dad was never around. My only interactions with other men involved some sort of destructive behavior. My family members forced me to fight kids from their neighborhood at a young age. Every one of them seemed to challenge my manhood, but no one helped me find it.

The fighting made me feel like an animal, a prop for their enjoyment. In their minds, they were saving me from being a "mama's boy," but I wasn't into it. I was sensitive, artistic, and fascinated by the creative. I bobbed my head when the radio played a song I liked, and I dissected the intricacies of each piece because I thought music was beautiful—which, of course, meant I was soft and less of a man in their eyes.

My adolescent world respected force and authority above all else, which only made me shrink back. I never responded like the tough gangster or courageous movie character everybody else wanted me to be. I always backed down or ran away. I was beaten, molested, and shamed by words no young man should have to hear. And each time, I ran away from the abuse—physically, mentally, emotionally—no matter how often it happened.

Music was my ticket out, my release, my path to the top. Performing was the only way I knew how to numb the pain until I couldn't feel it anymore. I was brave, and yet so broken. But slowly over the years, I have discovered that wounds have a harsh way of resurfacing when you numb them for too long. No amount of alcohol, pleasure, or medication would make mine go away. I knew eventually I had to face my wounds if I didn't want to feel so broken anymore. Someday, you will have to face your wounds and brokenness as well. So let's do this together.

What are some of the wounds you've experienced in your life and the ways you've felt broken?

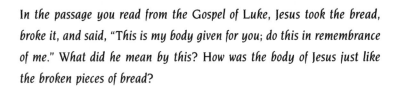

In the passage you read from the Gospel of Luke, Jesus took the bread, broke it, and said, "This is my body given for you; do this in remembrance of me." What did he mean by this? How was the body of Jesus just like the broken pieces of bread?

What do Peter and the prophet Isaiah mean when they say, "By his wounds we are healed" (1 Peter 2:24; Isaiah 53:5)?

What are the areas in your life where you are desperate for healing? How have the brokenness and wounds of Jesus been a healing message for you?

Pray: Talk with God about your own wounds and brokenness. Ask him to give you hope when you feel despair and healing when it seems impossible.

Day 2: Shake it Off

Read: Jonah 1–4; Luke 8:40–48

We are so wired to "fix" ourselves. We read books, listen to podcasts, attend conferences and seminars, and consume an insane amount of self-help material. We try hard to "shake it off," thinking the pain or the turmoil will disappear if we can just find the right fix for whatever we're going through. And if we grew up in the church, we likely participated in the common response to pain and trauma by *minimizing* it, *over-spiritualizing* it, or *memorializing* it.

While this response is meant to help, it actually does more harm. The truth is, we can only fix ourselves for so long before we need to get help from outside. *Yes, we need God's help.* But when we can't shake off what weighs us down, we also need help from specialists—people who are skilled and educated in medical science, health, and human services.

I know from my own experience that depression and anxiety are a dangerous force together and I simply couldn't continue to push through all of it on my own. The more I tried, the more I compounded the trauma and the more I grew numb. I needed a therapist, not a theologian—someone who could interpret my life and make sense of why I was walking through chaos without hope of escaping the tunnel. And here's what I learned: If we're ever going to get healthy, we have to actually turn and face our turmoil with the help of others.

We can't just shake it off on our own. We have to do it together. How did Jonah try to fix his own situation? How did that turn out for him?

The woman who touched the cloak of Jesus was sick for more than twelve years, but no one could heal her. What was it that finally healed her?

In what ways have you minimized, over-spiritualized, or memorialized your pain?

In what ways have you tried to "shake off" your own pain and turmoil?

Pray: Talk with God about the ways you've tried to shake off pain and turmoil on your own. Ask him to lead you to the next steps you need to take on your journey toward hope and healing.

Day 3: Searching for Hope

Read: Deuteronomy 6:1–12; Mark 12:28–34; Romans 5:1–8

Families shape our lives in ways we can't fully appreciate until we do the hard work of understanding the patterns that made us who we are. In my own life, family has always been a sore spot for me, a place of mixed results and feelings. It's been a place of influence and also a place of abuse and childhood trauma with a dangerous apathy towards pain and dysfunction.

While the wounds of my past motivated me to be the best possible husband and father I could be, they also created a sense of denial. When I came to Jesus, I was excited to gain a new family that would fill in the gaps I had felt in my childhood. And I was greeted by a host of father figures, mentors, sisters, and brothers who would walk with me in my faith journey. But I still needed healing from the wounds of my past. Without the hope of healing, I couldn't truly step into the true freedom I had received in Christ.

At one point, I convinced myself I had found healing in my relationship with God. But because I was still in denial about how my past was affecting my present, I was really just trying to earn the approval of God. It was a pattern that had served me well in childhood, but it felt empty to me as an adult. On stage, I appeared to be healed, unashamed, and restored. Yet in my private moments, without the applause and approval of a crowd, I would sit in silence and beg God to take away my shame and sense of worthlessness that stemmed from my past.

Eventually, in the silence, God whispered to me, "*I already have.*" God had already addressed my shame, my guilt, my shortcomings, and my healing. I just had to walk it out.

What holds you back from addressing difficult things from your family of origin?

Why is it so radical that Jesus expanded the original Old Testament command to love God to include "love your neighbor as yourself"?

How does loving God and loving others lead to hope and healing?

Paul states that we have hope in the glory of God and in the glory of our sufferings. What kind of hope have you found in God? What kind of hope has been found in your suffering?

Pray: Talk with God about your search for hope and healing. Ask him to help you find the courage you need to take hold of the hope and healing that he has waiting for you.

Day 4: Following God's Script

Read: Genesis 35:9–15; Genesis 41:1–57; Acts 9:1–43; Philippians 3:12–14

When I was at one of my lowest points, I spent a lot of mental energy searching for the right way to think or act my way out of the depression and anxiety I was feeling. The more my past affected me as a person, the more depressed and anxious I became, and the more these dangerous forces affected me as a parent and a spouse.

I was desperate for some kind of script or guide on how to live a better life. It was then I remembered reading the work of a professor who wrote about rules for priests in the Torah, the law of the Old Testament. He said there were detailed scripts of what the temple *priests* were supposed to do, and yet no specific rules in Scripture for being a *king*. This sunk deep within me. There was no script for how to rule, no script for how to lead, no script for a king's loyalty and duty in God's Word. As strange as it may sound, this gave me hope as a fatherless kid who was still looking for a father-figure, a role model, a family, and a place to belong.

I couldn't follow the family script that came from the violent or absent men in my life, but God had a script for me to follow and that gave me hope for my own healing. God's script was simply to love him completely and love others—love my family well, love my neighbors faithfully—and navigate life in light of these two commands. God's script was my way out of the darkness and back into the light. God's script was my roadmap to healing.

Both Jacob and Joseph had a troubled past, yet God turned their shame, regret, and failures into something good. What was God's "script" for Jacob? What was it for Joseph?

God had a script for Paul as well. How does understanding the context of Paul's conversion story in Acts bring greater clarity to his words, "Forgetting what is behind and straining toward what is ahead, I press on . . ." (Philippians 3:13)?

In what ways have you experienced the script God has for you? What stories or verses from the Bible stand out to you and keep you moving forward regardless of your past?

Pray: Talk with God about the script that he has for you. Ask him to help you "forget" what is behind you so you can press toward the life ahead that he has in store for you.

Day Five: Pursuing Healing

Read: Mark 10:46–52; Luke 19:1–10; 1 John 1:5–10

At my lowest point, I remember crying out, "God, I am emotionally and relationally broken. Lead me to the people and the processes that will bring about healing." And he did.

Now, this wasn't immediate. And it took some time before I found my footing and could actually say that I was on the road to healing. But I definitely sensed God's presence was with me as I took steps to pursue healing. First, I needed to own up to and confess the denial I had about my destructive behavior and the reality of my depression and anxiety. Then, I needed to pause and reconnect with God, with myself, and with my wife.

We took a vacation just to catch our breath together. That is when I realized the severity of my depression and anxiety. Two steps forward felt like three steps back, as I had a panic attack while just chilling out in our hotel room. That episode was my catalyst for taking a much-needed sabbatical from work. Pursuing healing meant I had to face who I was without the fame and recognition of being on tour or collaborating with music greats I adored. I had to face how my past was affecting my present and how my body was responding to the pain of my past even when my mind was telling me I was okay.

This led me to take the steps necessary to get the help I needed. I found a good therapist and started taking care of my body, getting the rest I needed, and being consistent with exercise, medication, and healthy food. And here's what I learned in the process: Healing doesn't happen on its own. Healing requires action. That's why I talk about my pursuit of healing: confessing, pausing, reconnecting, and taking necessary steps to get healthy.

How did Bartimaeus pursue physical healing? How did Jesus respond to him?

How did Zacchaeus pursue spiritual healing? How did Jesus respond to him?

What role does confession play in our pursuit of healing?

In what ways will you choose to "live in the light" and pursue healing today?

Pray: Talk with God about your pursuit of healing. Ask him to help you find your footing by confessing, pausing, reconnecting, and taking the necessary steps toward healing.

For Next Week

Use the space below to write any insights or questions that you want to discuss at the next group meeting. In preparation for next week, read chapters 3–5 in I Am Restored.

Confronting the Chaos

You are no longer foreigners and strangers,
but fellow citizens with God's people
and also members of his household.
EPHESIANS 2:19

Welcome

It is a sad fact of history that the church doesn't always represent Jesus well. From the genocide of native peoples, to the promotion of slavery, to the Jim Crow laws and other forms of oppression, the church has often been just as guilty as our society as a whole. Most of us interact with church through our own experiences and, for this reason, we may not even be familiar with some of these historical events or the misinformed theology behind them. Much of our understanding of God has been shaped by the version of Christianity we find most appealing, or the version we were strongly encouraged to accept by our family of origin.

As with many black Americans, I grew up with a deep bloodline in the traditional black church. But college drastically changed my perception of what church and faith could be for me. I knew I loved Jesus and urban culture, but I needed something to intellectually stimulate me. I was committed to finding the church culture where I fit in, so I explored many expressions of the Christian tradition until I found one that seemed to fit best for me: the conservative evangelical (and predominantly white) church space.

This eventually led to a disdain for the black church for a season. Looking back, I realize I was blinded by my own arrogance and ignorance of black church practices. I completely missed the theological rootedness of the black church, because I was so intent on being intellectually and theologically "right." Soon I was weaving reformed theology into my lyrics—and the conservative evangelical (also, predominantly white) Christian crowd loved it.

But as my art started to expand, so did my theology. I began to see subtle double-standards in the music business, in church (not to mention church history), and in politics regarding racial justice. But when I spoke out about those injustices and double standards, I was rejected by my tribe in hurtful ways. It pained me to also hear that many people in the black Christian community saw me as a sellout or a "mascot" for the white Christian community.

My deconstructing faith, mixed with the reality of American politics and ever-growing racial injustice splattered across the news, was the perfect storm of chaos. I realized that I had spent so much of my life meeting the cultural expectations of other Christians based on minor teachings of the Bible rather than on the major commands of loving God and others. I knew something had to change. I *had* to confront the chaos.

Share

If you or any of your group members are just getting to know one another, take a few minutes to introduce yourselves and share any insights you have from last week's personal study. Then, to kick things off, discuss one of the following questions:

- Can you name one or two ways that you experienced chaos—either individually or collectively?

  —*or*—

- What word would you use to describe the chaos you have experienced?

Read

Invite someone to read aloud Matthew 5:1–12. Listen for fresh insights as you hear the verses being read, and then discuss the questions that follow.

¹ Now when Jesus saw the crowds, he went up on a mountainside and sat down. His disciples came to him, ² and he began to teach them.
He said:

³ "Blessed are the poor in spirit,
    for theirs is the kingdom of heaven.
⁴ Blessed are those who mourn,
    for they will be comforted.
⁵ Blessed are the meek,

for they will inherit the earth.

[6] Blessed are those who hunger and thirst for
righteousness,
for they will be filled.

[7] Blessed are the merciful,
for they will be shown mercy.

[8] Blessed are the pure in heart,
for they will see God.

[9] Blessed are the peacemakers,
for they will be called children of God.

[10] Blessed are those who are persecuted because
of righteousness,
for theirs is the kingdom of heaven.

[11] "Blessed are you when people insult you, persecute you and falsely say all kinds of evil against you because of me. [12] Rejoice and be glad, because great is your reward in heaven, for in the same way they persecuted the prophets who were before you."

Look at the list of people Jesus names as being "blessed." What stands out to you about them?

Why do you think people in our world today tend to not consider these types of people as "blessed"—or even want to be like them?

The Context

This passage is about Jesus addressing the justice issues of his day. He is "turning the tables" on the definition of righteousness regarding those who will enter the kingdom of heaven—in a way that astonishes his audience. This passage represents the turning point in the ministry of Jesus. It is the moment he declared himself to be the fulfillment of Old Testament prophecies concerning the Messiah and publicly disagreed with the Pharisees—the religious leaders of the day who were still marginalizing people with their religious rules and regulations.

Watch

Play the video segment for session two (see the streaming video access provided on the inside front cover). As you watch, use the following outline to record any thoughts or concepts that stand out to you.

Discovering church

Encountering the message of the gospel

Attempting to bridge the gap between church experiences

Chaos in the church

Speaking out against injustice in society

Response of the church and the lack of empathy

Chaos in society

Political ideology shows up the church

Lack of empathy from Christian leaders for systemic racism

Abandoning the faith

A people wound became a God wound

Taking off the armor and throwing caution to the wind

Without hope, it's hard to heal

Finding the way back

Rediscovering the wisdom of the black church

Finding a global perspective of God

Serving when you don't know what to say

Addiction to religion

Jesus challenged the Pharisees, who ignored the needs of people

Addicted to looking good while ignoring the people who need God's love

Character Study

In the Bible, we read many stories about Jesus's interactions with a group known as the Pharisees. The name likely comes from a Hebrew word meaning "separate" or "detach," which describes their philosophy—they wished to adhere strictly to the Law of Moses and be separate from other groups. They pursued purity with a passion and were the religious leaders of the day.

Unfortunately, the Gospels also make it clear that they were the *legalistic* leaders of the day. In Luke 5:17–39, we find the Pharisees watching Jesus's every move as he taught the crowds, healed a paralyzed man, and ate in the home of a despised tax collector. They accuse Jesus of blasphemy when he heals the paralyzed man. They accuse him of uncleanliness by eating and drinking with sinners. They question his religious authority because his followers did not fast the way the Pharisees expect them to fast. Each time, Jesus brought their accusations back to the dignity and the humanity of the people present in each story.

Jesus not only healed the paralyzed man but also told him that his sins had been forgiven. Jesus responded to the Pharisees' questions about eating in a home with social outcasts by saying, "It is not the healthy who need a doctor, but the sick" (verse 31). And he made an allowance for the disciples regarding the laws of fasting, knowing they would once again fast in accordance with religious laws when he was no longer in their presence.

It's easy to see how Jesus put the needs of others above his own and above the approval of the religious leaders of the day. He saw people who were longing to be seen and heard—people who felt as though they had no voice. The question is . . . are we willing to do the same? Following in the footsteps of Jesus and standing up on behalf of others is part of the journey toward restoration.

Discuss

Take a few minutes with your group members to discuss what you just watched and explore these concepts in Scripture. Then take time to pray together as a group. Use the space at the end of this session to keep track of prayer requests and group updates.

1. What stood out to you from listening to Lecrae today? How can you identify with the stories he shared?

2. Lecrae talked about his different church experiences after he had come to faith in Christ as a teenager. How can you relate to his story of experiencing diverse church communities? What kind of impact did those church experiences have on you?

3. Many Christians today are "addicted to religion" in that they are more devoted to their devotion than they are to God. The same was true of the Pharisees in Jesus's day. Read Matthew 23:1–7. What are some of the traits that Jesus calls out about the Pharisees? How do you see these same traits at work in the church today?

4. It is a sad reality that those who choose to step up, go against the norm, and speak out for causes near to God's heart are often met with criticism. In what ways was this true in Lecrae's story? How have you found this to be true in your own story?

5. The apostle Paul wrote that "if anyone is in Christ, the new creation has come: the old has gone, the new is here!" (2 Corinthians 5:17). Lecrae discussed how his faith was made "new" by the hope and healing he found in Jesus. In what ways can you relate to his story? How have you experienced the new life that Jesus came to provide to you?

6. Lecrae offered a few words of encouragement at the end of this week's teaching regarding how to confront chaos in the church. How will you respond to these words? What steps will you take to continue the fight toward racial justice?

Respond

Briefly review the outline for the video teaching and any notes you took. In the space below, write down the most significant point you took away from this session.

Pray

Pray as a group before you close your time together. Thank God for the way that Jesus addresses your chaos with compassion. Thank him for always seeing you as a new creation in Christ—regardless of your past or present. Ask him to continue to give you the courage to confront the chaos that rises up in your life.

Between-Sessions Personal Study

Reflect on the material you covered during this week's group time by engaging in the following personal studies. Each day offers a short reading adapted from I Am Restored, along with a few reflection questions to take you deeper into the theme of this week's study. Be sure to read the reflection questions and make a few notes in your guide about the experience. At the start of your next session, you will have a few minutes to share any insights that you learned.

Day 1: The Chaos of Church Hurt

Read: Mark 12:1–37; Luke 10:25–37; Luke 15:11–32

I think many Christians today unfortunately suffer with an "addiction to religion." Christianity is a faith with a set of beliefs that include rituals and rules. But the problem is not with those beliefs, rituals, and rules—it is with the cultural practices we've baptized in biblical language. I'm guilty of this, too. My works and self-righteousness became badges I wore to parade how right I was. I wanted to *appear* good instead of *be* good. I wanted to be seen as wise and faithful, especially to the theological gatekeepers of my particular brand of the Christian faith.

This type of devotion-to-devotion, rather than devotion-to-God, was displayed by the Pharisees who opposed Jesus. They wanted to parade around and show everyone how good they were by the rules they kept. Confronting the chaos in my life meant that I had to come to the painful realization that I *was just like them.* I wasn't devoted to God. I was devoted to my devotion of a Western view of faith.

So I began to explore diverse perspectives and interrogate my own faith. But this only drove a wedge between me and my church tribe. Ultimately, I found myself exhausted from living as the representative of a group that didn't really accept me for who I was. The pressure to maintain appearances and accept cultural elements of American Christianity that didn't acknowledge my black heritage with dignity started to sour on me as I stepped into more mainstream settings with my music and more diverse spaces with my voice. I was unprepared for the chaotic behavior from fellow Christians—betrayal, backbiting, marginalization, embarrassment, shame, even spiritual abuse—and the church hurt that followed.

Church hurt is the worst kind of dysfunction for the person who believes the church is serious about their invitation to "come as you are." I am no longer willing to accept a Christian expression of faith that refuses to hear voices from the margins. The Christian body is far more global, eclectic, and diverse than we are comfortable in admitting. I'm living proof that you can confront the chaos of church hurt and still seek a faith-filled community of other believers.

What are some ways you've experienced or contributed to the chaos of church hurt?

What do you notice about the way Jesus responds to the Pharisees who condemn his actions? How does this kind of religious mindset show up in the church today?

What is the point of the Good Samaritan story told by Jesus? How did Samaritans and other Gentiles experience church hurt from the Jews?

Lecrae mentions how he identifies with the younger son in the story of the Prodigal Son, returning to the love and freedom of Jesus despite the chaos of his life. Which character is you: the younger son, the older son, or the father? Why?

Pray: Talk with God about the chaos you see in church today, asking forgiveness for any of the ways you've contributed to church hurt. Ask God to give you a faith community like the father gave to his prodigal son—one with open arms, a safe place to wrestle, and unconditional love.

Day 2: The Chaos of Injustice

Read: Exodus 5:1–6:8; Acts 15:22–35; Galatians 3:1–29

Like most black Americans, I don't know much about my family's history. Most black families avoid sharing intimate details of our lineage for many reasons. We don't have the privilege of tracing our ancestors back to a specific country or region with any certainty. But we know enough to be enraged by the racial injustice we've experienced and the centuries of silence toward racism both inside and outside the church.

As I started to speak out against the chaos of injustice that I witnessed around me, church leaders started referring to me and my peers as "social justice warriors." They jumped to conclusions about our influences and branded us in public for other followers to see. But from my perspective, the American church was late to the party in condemning racism, and that was a painful experience for me and my peers of color who called the church our home.

I felt a mixture of pain and relief as I was pushed away by church leaders and friends and, at the same time, began to pull away on my own. Beyond losing a sense of security, I felt like the white American church had turned its back on me, which only perpetuated what I always knew to be true: Racism will always find you. It's a systemic evil baked into the fabric of our country, and if you don't proactively dismantle racism, it will find its way to you.

All across America today, there's a collective sense of anguish and grief in communities of color who hold the pain and trauma of racism in their bodies. I started to wonder about the cost of this collective trauma. Slowly, I realized that the most important question I could ask myself wasn't whether *white evangelicalism cared about black bodies but whether God saw this evil, heard our cries, and cares about black bodies.* I had doubts about the answer to these questions. But those doubts made me realize I had so much to unlearn about my discipleship experience in order to get to the answer.

In the midst of the chaos of injustice, I found a God who is near to the oppressed, who grieves when we grieve, and who cares about racial justice. It's plain to see in the Bible that God has plenty to say about disenfranchised and overlooked communities. Racism has existed for thousands of years, and it's evil—but it's not bigger than death. Jesus has already defeated death and confronted the chaos of injustice. And we get to carry out the work he started.

How have you witnessed the chaos of racial injustice in your life, in your faith community, or in society? (Be specific with your examples. Labeling difficult emotions and experiences is a way to let them inform you instead of overwhelm you. You need to name it to tame it.)

What kind of injustices did the Israelites experience at the hand of the Egyptians in the story you read from Exodus? How did God respond to these injustices?

The apostle Paul records the deliberation of Jewish leaders in Acts regarding the acceptance of Gentiles into the Christian faith. In what ways does our Western expression of faith still sound like the Jews who wanted to make the Gentiles follow Christ in certain Jewish ways?

What steps can you take to start living the Jesus-centered theology we see in Galatians 3:28, where Paul says, "There is neither Jew nor Gentile, neither slave nor free, nor is there male and female, for you are all one in Christ Jesus"?

Pray: Talk with God about his view of the injustices you see in our world. Thank him for the salvation and freedom that Jesus provided to ALL people through his death on the cross.

Day 3: Course-Correcting the Chaos

Read: Matthew 12:1–37; Isaiah 42:1–9; Matthew 18:15–20

Many people don't feel they need to understand or embrace the nuances of chaos in other sectors of society because their lives aren't directly affected by those nuances. But choosing not to confront the chaos is a *privilege.* I believe that Jesus would be course-correcting our chaos by addressing important issues that affect every sphere of life.

Privilege, especially political privilege, is the ability to not care about certain issues because they don't directly affect you or because you don't have categories to explain them. Your perspective often depends on your proximity to those issues. Does your life regularly intersect with people who are different from you? Do you understand the chaos they are going through—the hurt and the pain in their lives? If not, then you need to course-correct your response to chaos.

In I Am *Restored*, I tell the story of a diverse group of teenagers standing on the sideline of a soccer field. Each one is prompted to take a step forward according to certain life situations, such as having two parents at home, having parents with a college education, and having families that are free of drugs, substance abuse, and incarceration. At the end of the questions, many of the students of color are far behind the white students.

Examples like this make me wonder how we will ever achieve equity if one group starts so far ahead of another. But I think it's possible to course-correct if we are willing to consider the depth of our own privilege. We all have an opportunity to use our influence to create more just and equitable systems, to prioritize voices of color, and to enter into shared experiences with solidarity and humility. This is also where the church can course-correct—by discipling with empathy, solidarity, and humility.

On a scale of 1 to 10 (1 being low, 10 being high), how would you rate your participation in course-correcting the political, social, theological, and racial justice around you? Why did you give yourself that rating?

How has your privilege or lack of privilege influenced your participation in social causes?

Matthew and Isaiah remind us that one of Jesus's priorities on earth was to bring about justice. What are some of the ways that Jesus succeeded in doing this?

In Matthew 18:15–20, Jesus provides us with several steps to take when we experience injustice. First, we address the offenders one-on-one. If they refuse to admit their fault, we lovingly confront them with a witness or two. Second, if that doesn't work, we take the matter to the leadership of our church or our community. Third, if they still refuse to acknowledge or apologize for their behavior, we set boundaries so no further harm can be done. How will you use this example to address injustice and course-correct the chaos you see around you?

Pray: Talk with God about your position of privilege or non-privilege and what that means to you. Ask God to help you see the responsibility and the call of Jesus to help course-correct the injustices of the world today—beginning with the situations and circumstances closest to you.

Day 4: The Justice of Jesus

Read: Deuteronomy 32:1–4; Psalm 89:1–18; Micah 6:6–8; Luke 4:14–20

We started talking about the justice of Jesus during our last exercise on course-correcting the chaos. But it would be a big mistake to simply move on from there. It's important to understand that the justice of Jesus is actually the justice of God. All throughout the Old Testament, we read about the justice of God. And in the Gospels, we read about the justice of Jesus. It's easy to separate the two, but what if we paid closer attention to the connection? What if we saw the life of God in the life of Jesus, especially as it relates to justice?

Justice of any kind matters, but I believe addressing racial justice is crucial for the future of America and the future of the church in America. If racial justice mattered to God and mattered to Jesus, then it should matter to us as well. When we look closely at the context of Jesus's stories about healing the sick, feeding the poor, and bringing freedom to the oppressed, more often than not, there was also a racial justice component to these stories.

The same goes for stories about the rescue and the redemption of God. The Israelites' exodus out of Egypt was about racial justice. The story of Daniel in the lions' den was about racial justice. The stories about the Gentiles and the Jews are about racial justice. If we dig deep and understand these stories in their original context, we see that the thread of racial justice runs throughout the entire Bible.

The justice and the love of God go together (see Luke 11:42). If we start paying attention to this fact, we begin to see how crucial this is to our lives as Christians. We may also learn to lament the ways that we've experienced racial injustice or contributed to racial injustice in the past. This creates space for us to grieve and take responsibility for any part we may have played in the pain of others. And the justice of Jesus gives us a pathway for leading ourselves and others on the journey of racial justice awareness and action.

Have you ever considered the idea that we see the justice of God in the justice of Jesus?

How is Jesus the fulfillment of the justice of God?

According to Luke 4:14–20, what are some ways that Jesus carried out justice during his time on earth? Can you give specific instances found in Scripture that illustrate this list of examples?

How has Lecrae's story inspired you to "act justly, love mercy and walk humbly" with God? What specific steps will you take toward justice this week?

Pray: Talk with God today about this issue of justice that you read about in the Bible. Ask him to help you find the courage to take responsibility and action on the journey toward racial justice.

Day 5: You Get to Choose

Read: Acts 15:1–21; Ephesians 4:1–16; Romans 12:9–21; James 1:19–27

Let's circle back to something I said earlier in this session: *church hurt is the worst kind of hurt.* My heart breaks for those who believe the invitation of thousands of churches to "come as you are," only to find out that's not actually what the church meant—it was simply the slogan they used to get you inside the door. But here's what I want you to hear from me: *you get to choose.*

You get to choose where to put down roots in a faith community, where to show up with your family on a Saturday evening or Sunday morning, and where to gather around the table with other believers for intentional conversation about what you're learning about life and from the Bible. And you don't have to stay in one place, if the place you've been showing up is no longer a safe space for you.

When I started speaking out against the chaos and racial injustice that I saw happening around me and across the nation, my church community started to shut me down and push me out. This was painful, but it was the catalyst I needed to find a faith community that cared about the things I imagined God cared about, including racial justice. I got to choose where I wanted to invest my time, my energy, and my commitment in community with other faithful followers of Jesus. And you have this same choice.

So, if your church no longer seems like a safe place because of their response to your brokenness, or denial of their own chaos, or indifference to justice, you have the freedom to find another place to worship. Now, remember that *there are no perfect churches out there.* So, don't look for perfection. But do look for a community that reflects the heart of God in a way that aligns with the love and justice of God. Just be willing to take that first step.

What was the big dispute among Jewish Christians regarding Gentile Christians in Acts 15:1–21? How did the Jews make things right with the Gentiles? Why did this matter to God?

How would you summarize Paul's instructions to the Ephesians about how to be a church—the "body of Christ"? Which instruction stands out to you? Why?

How well does your faith community reflect Paul's description of "love in action" (Romans 12:9–21)? Where could it improve? How can you contribute to making those improvements?

According to James 1:19–27, what does active religion look like? How would you rate your church on these specific actions? How would you rate yourself on these actions?

Pray: Talk with God today about your own community of faith. Ask for his continued leading to be part of a group of believers that represents his values to the world.

For Next Week

Use the space below to write any insights or questions that you want to discuss at the next group meeting. In preparation for next week, read chapters 6–7 in I Am Restored.

Discovering Hope

"For I know the plans I have for you," declares
the Lord, "plans to prosper you and not to harm
you, plans to give you a hope and a future."
JEREMIAH 29:11

Welcome

Uncovering the wounds of my childhood left me confused and in
pain. I was traumatized from decades of rejection. All I wanted
was be affirmed by people who loved *all* of me. But I felt trapped
in a cycle of bondage. Sin was the only thing that felt like it could
numb my pain. But the sin led to shame, and that shame brought
on a current of deep depression.

I never imagined I would end up that far gone, but that's the
way chaos works. Dysfunction has a tendency to creep up on us
when we least expect it. Everything changed when I realized I
wasn't just in a dysfunctional state—I was battling legit depression. And my poor decisions and self-medication only made my

situation worse than it already was. Mild depression spiraled into clinical depression for three straight months. In the midst of this crisis, I realized that talking about depression in church, of all places, was taboo.

Some Christians will tell you that mental illness can be overcome with theology or by praying the right prayer. Certainly, we read in the Bible that "the prayer offered in faith will make the sick person well" and that "the prayer of a righteous person is powerful and effective" (James 5:15–16). We read how Peter brought healing to a lame man in Jerusalem (see Acts 3:1–10) and how Paul did the same in Lystra (see Acts 14:8–10). But when that doesn't happen in your life, those who are depressed sink even deeper into darkness.

The road of discipleship is littered with broken souls ripped apart by their fear to face depression with compassionate hearts. And without compassion, the pain is overwhelming. The loud message is that those who struggle with depression have to figure it out on their own.

I know because I've been there. I felt lost and without hope—like a superhero who had all their power sapped from them by the villain. I was at the peak of my mainstream music career, but at the same time I was deeply sick. To make matters worse, I didn't know what to believe about God anymore. I was trapped in the bondage of despair, and this cycle was happening in front of the world. That is . . . until I took a much-needed break and started asking God to make himself real to me.

After a trip to Egypt with my wife, where we saw the story of Jesus through the lens of Coptic Christians, and a few experiences where God spoke to me in some direct and dramatic ways, I found myself feeling hopeful again. And this spark was fueled even further by my close friendships. I was finding my way out of the depression and despair by discovering hope.

Share

Begin your group time by inviting those in the group to share their insights from last week's personal study. Then, to kick things off, discuss one of the following questions:

- Can you name a few ways confronting chaos creates a way for finding hope?

— o r —

- What keeps you going when you are feeling low?

Read

Invite someone to read aloud 1 Kings 19:1–8, 15–18. Listen for fresh insights as you hear the verses being read, and then discuss the questions that follow.

[1] Now Ahab told Jezebel everything Elijah had done and how he had killed all the prophets with the sword. [2] So Jezebel sent a messenger to Elijah to say, "May the gods deal with me, be it ever so severely, if by this time tomorrow I do not make your life like that of one of them."

[3] Elijah was afraid and ran for his life. When he came to Beersheba in Judah, he left his servant there, [4] while he himself went a day's journey into the wilderness. He came to a broom bush, sat down under it and prayed that he might die. "I have had enough, LORD," he said. "Take my life; I am no better than my ancestors." [5] Then he lay down under the bush and fell asleep.

All at once an angel touched him and said, "Get up and eat." [6] He looked around, and there by his head was some bread baked over hot coals, and a jar of water. He ate and drank and then lay down again.

[7] The angel of the LORD came back a second time and touched him and said, "Get up and eat, for the journey is too much for you." [8] So he got up and ate and drank. Strengthened by that food, he traveled forty days and forty nights until he reached Horeb, the mountain of God. . . .

[15] The LORD said to him, "Go back the way you came, and go to the Desert of Damascus. When you get there, anoint Hazael king over Aram. [16] Also, anoint Jehu son of Nimshi king over Israel, and anoint Elisha son of Shaphat from Abel Meholah to succeed you as prophet. [17] Jehu will put to death any who escape the sword of Hazael, and Elisha will put to death any who escape the sword of Jehu. [18] Yet I reserve seven thousand in Israel—all whose knees have not bowed down to Baal and whose mouths have not kissed him."

What insights do you notice about Elijah? How would you describe his state of mind?

How did God reassure Elijah that he was not alone in his struggle?

The Context

As the events of this story unfold, Elijah has just witnessed an incredible victory on the top of Mount Carmel. He had set up a duel of sorts with the prophets of Baal to see who was more powerful—their god or *the* God. The priests of Baal called on their god from morning until noon to light an altar, but to no avail. Then, after one prayer from Elijah, the Lord rained down fire from heaven, incinerating the sacrifice, the wood, the stones, and the soil around it. The Israelites quickly lost faith in Baal and followed Elijah's guidance in trusting the Lord. But it only took a rumor shortly after that Queen Jezebel was after his head to cause Elijah to flee. He had been obedient to God and just witnessed a powerful miracle, yet he still ran away in fear. Elijah was a mighty man of God . . . but also human like us.

Watch

Play the video segment for session three (see the streaming video access provided on the inside front cover). As you watch, use the following outline to record any thoughts or concepts that stand out to you.

Finding hope in the midst of a faith crisis

Wrestling with life in the spotlight

The guilt of going too far to turn back

Understanding mental health

Dealing with acute anxiety

Discovering God during a breakdown

Fear of rejection from community

There is freedom in confession and suffering in suppression

The greatest gift of friends and family

Facing depression with God

Healing requires hope, and hope requires hearing from God

God gives us plans and a promise (see Jeremiah 29:11)

To make it through the pain, we have to hold onto the promise of God

Taking a sabbatical: sitting still gives time to just "be"

Rebuilding our lives requires embracing a new reality

Character Study

The story of Samson is told in Judges 13–16. Even before Samson was born, he was destined to be a mighty warrior. Samson's destiny was prophesied to his mother by an angel of the Lord who said Samson would be a Nazarite and deliver Israel from the Philistines. The vow of a Nazarite was voluntary and for a period of time, but this was not the case for Samson. He was to be a Nazarite for *life*.

This meant that Samson was required to follow certain restrictions regarding the food he ate. He was also not allowed to cut his hair with a razor, which meant that he lived most of his life with long locks. In exchange, God gave Samson exceptional physical strength.

Over time, Samson violated every restriction that came with being a Nazarite. He chose a Philistine wife against the wishes of his family. He violated a Nazarite rule to avoid dead bodies by eating honey out of the carcass of a young lion. He gambled away clothes he did not have during his own wedding feast, and then took innocent Philistine lives to pay back the debt. In retaliation, the Philistines killed his wife, which prompted Samson to singlehandedly declare war on the Philistines. Yet in spite of these violations, God was merciful toward him.

Eventually, in order to defend his people, Samson turned himself in to the Philistines. They tied him up, but he broke the ropes and escaped. Samson later returned to Philistine territory, where he met a woman named Delilah. She was approached by the Philistine leaders to uncover the source of Samson's strength and was able to learn from Samson that if his head were shaved, his strength would leave him and he would be as weak as any other man.

Samson's head was shaved, and this time his strength left him. But in his final hours, as Lecrae notes in this session, he prayed for the Lord to return his strength—and God answered. "Thus he killed many more when he died than while he lived" (Judges 16:30). Yet the story of Samson is a sad one—a tale of what might have been. Just imagine how much more effective Samson would have been if he had honored God with his *whole* life. In the same way, just image how God could use our lives if we surrendered ourselves wholly and completely to him.

Discuss

Take a few minutes with your group members to discuss what you just watched and explore these concepts in Scripture.

1. What stood out to you from listening to Lecrae today? How can you identify with Lecrae's need for a break from life?

2. Each of us will go through times in this life when we feel discouraged, frustrated, and even hopeless. Read Psalm 88:6–14. In these verses, the psalmist expresses the despair that he is feeling and voices it to God. When have you likewise felt that you were going through "the lowest pit in the darkest depths"?

3. How has it helped you to express these feelings to God? How did the Lord meet you in those moments when you cried out to him?

4. Lecrae noted the importance of having good friends around him as he fought his way through doubt and depression. How has your community loved you and encouraged you in this same way as you have gone through struggles in your life?

5. Jesus said to his disciples, "Peace I leave with you; my peace I give you. I do not give to you as the world gives. Do not let your hearts be troubled and do not be afraid" (John 14:27). How have you witnessed this peace from God during your darkest times? Why is it so critical to hold fast to God's promises when you are feeling despair?

6. Lecrae states in the teaching, "For us to make it through the pain, we have to hold on to the promise of hope. But in order to hold on to the promise, we have to spend time with the promise-maker." How are you making it a priority each day to spend time with God? How has spending this time with God helped you see his purpose for your life?

Respond

Briefly review the outline for the video teaching and any notes you took. In the space below, write down the most significant point you took away from this session.

Pray

Pray as a group before you close your time together. Thank God for making himself real to you through prayer, experiences, and the presence of close friends. Ask God for a glimmer of hope when you feel despair—and that you will sense his presence during those dark times.

Between-Sessions Personal Study

Reflect on the material you covered during this week's group time by engaging in the following personal studies. Each day offers a short reading adapted from I Am Restored, along with a few reflection questions to take you deeper into the theme of this week's study. Be sure to read the reflection questions and make a few notes in your guide about the experience. At the start of your next session, you will have a few minutes to share any insights that you learned.

Day 1: Diagnosing Depression

Read: 1 Kings 19:1–9; Matthew 6:25–34; Philippians 4:1–9

Even with all the warning signs, hitting rock bottom was still a surprise to me. I couldn't believe I woke up in a clinical depression. And I was constantly asking myself, *How did I get here?* Many of us are in a place where we know the bottom is falling out, but we can't put a name on it. We can't feel anything. We can't sleep. We can't eat . . . or we can't stop eating. We don't know how much more we can take, so we just find coping mechanisms.

For me, it was alcohol and pills, but for others it's shopping, gossiping about others, becoming hyper-focused and rigid in our religious ways, pursuing adventure after adventure, indulging or obsessing about food, and so on. Most of us don't know that we're coping. We can't recognize that our obsessive behaviors are actually addictions that empower us to avoid our deeper issues. Then we ignore how serious they are to justify ourselves. We are determined to make it through our depression, anxiety, and hardships by any means necessary.

Instead of speaking clearly and openly about my depression and my emotions—something I never felt free to do growing up—I turned to coping mechanisms to numb myself from the need to express whatever I was feeling. This is where I found myself in the middle of this cycle of depression. At that point, I was close to the cliff of leaping off into the hedonistic culture of celebrity life. But I knew I would never be happy following that pattern of living. I felt *nothing* but wanted to feel *something*.

I would imagine we've all experienced depression in some form at some stage of our lives. But I'm here to tell you that numbing out will only create more chaos. God has a purpose for your pain, if you're willing to take an honest look at what's ailing you and take the necessary steps to get the help you need. This isn't weakness. Owning up to the way our emotions affect us is actually a strength. Restoration requires us to let go of the ways that no longer serve God's purpose for our lives. And, yes, sometimes restoration looks like diagnosing depression.

As you reread 1 Kings 19:1–9, what signs do you see that Elijah was wrestling with depression? Has there ever been a time when you have wrestled with depression?

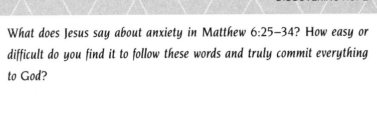
What does Jesus say about anxiety in Matthew 6:25–34? How easy or difficult do you find it to follow these words and truly commit everything to God?

How does Paul encourage the Philippians to combat anxiety? According to him, what happens when we push against anxiety with prayer?

How have you experienced the peace of God in the midst of depression, anxiety, or darkness in your life or in the lives of others?

Pray: Talk with God about the ways you have wrestled with the darkness of depression and anxiety. Ask for him to bring his peace to calm your heart and mind in miraculous ways.

Day 2: Rediscovering God

Read: Psalm 73:1–28; Job 42:1–6; John 20:19–29

During my spiral of depression, my journey with God grew more complicated. All of my default moves and disciplines weren't working. I felt spiritually malnourished, and I stopped maintaining any regular pattern of devotion. I stopped being attuned to where my heart was. I didn't have much hope that my love for God would ever come back.

The depression was dangerous, but my spiritual condition was deadly. I would ask myself, *If I didn't have my faith, who would I be?* Occasionally I threw out some prayers and read a few verses of Scripture, but my faith was nothing like before my depression or when I first started following Christ.

Before one of my shows, I was desperate for God to be real to me. I prayed for something I could feel, touch, and interact with—some signs that God hadn't completely abandoned me like my earthly father did. When I finished praying, I felt empty. That was it. If God didn't speak to me, then I was done. I was going to leave the faith.

But then God showed up in a random conversation I had backstage that same night with an Eastern Orthodox priest. And then, God started showing up in more ways than I could count. These random occurrences became more common. I would bump into people who had answers to the deep, dark questions I held inside. I even had dreams where I sensed God speaking to me. God kept showing me how real he was in simple and mysterious ways. Each and every time I struggled to believe that God was real, he would prove his realness to me.

God was opening the "closet" of my trauma and giving me the tools and support I needed to confront the chaos and discover a new sense of hope. He was turning my pain into purpose as he guided me back home to him. Rediscovering hope meant rediscovering God.

Why did the psalmist say that he had almost lost his foothold? How have you slipped away from God due to anxiety, depression, feeling overwhelmed, or numbing the pain in your life?

The psalmist goes on to say, "But as for me, it is good to be near God" (Psalm 73:28). How has this been true in your life?

What difference did it make for Job to not only hear God, but also to see God (see Job 42:5)? How has God made himself real to you, like he did for Job and the psalmist?

Even the disciple Thomas struggled to believe in the resurrection until he saw Christ and could place his fingers in the wounds on Jesus's hands. Now, we may not actually see Jesus, but we can experience Jesus in the presence of the people whom he has placed in our lives. Who has made the love of Jesus more real to you simply by being your friend or by showing up with an encouraging word or deed when you were in doubt? What impact did that have on you?

Pray: Talk with God about the ways that he has made himself real to you even in the midst of your own doubt, darkness, and despair. Ask him to continue to help you hear his voice and see him at work in the lives and love of the people around you.

Day 3: Presence over Performance

Read: Ephesians 2:1–10; 1 Corinthians 4:1–8; Proverbs 16:1–9

Everything in life pushes us to perform. Our social media timeline tells us we're not enough. Our families have expectations we fail to meet. Our employers evaluate our performance with consequences if we fail to meet our quotas. When the same mindset creeps into our relationship with Jesus, it corrupts our hearts and leads us to self-righteousness or despair.

Self-righteousness was the root of my ills. I was committed to loving my service to God rather than loving how God had already served me. All this time that I had followed Jesus and proclaimed how unashamed I was, I had missed the core motivation of serving him. The problem of my life wasn't that my actions were always immoral or wrong. But I was taking every opportunity to prove myself to others, and worse, to prove myself to God. I wanted to show God that I was "back on the right track." But I sacrificed presence for performance.

Everything about my shift back to Christianity and my transformation in Jesus was about proving myself and my devotion to God. I went back to constructing the same self-righteous structures that had defined my early walk with God prior to my road to healing. It wasn't that reading the Bible and revisiting old discipleship tools were wrong, but I was going through those motions not to have communion with God but to be accepted by him.

I wasn't fully healed, obviously, but I was in the process of healing. It would take me a few more rounds of performance fatigue before I realized the only pathway to true healing and freedom is radical transparency with the people who love you the most—including God. I had to stop performing and start being still. When

I did this, the glimmer of hope I had desperately searched for was present, and I could see the light at the end of the tunnel. But the presence of hope required my own personal presence—my presence instead of my performance.

The apostle Paul writes in Ephesians about faith versus works because of his Jewish heritage—he was used to following the rules and regulations of the Torah. How did faith in Jesus set Paul free from the performance-driven expectations of his culture?

How does the gift of salvation in Jesus set you free from living according to our performance-driven culture?

Paul also says the Lord will "bring to light what is hidden in darkness" and "expose the motives of the heart" (1 Corinthians 4:5). What is "hidden in darkness" in your life right now? Use a few descriptive words to explain what God sees when he looks at the motives of your heart right now. How is God shining a light on those dark places in your life?

What plans will you commit to the Lord as you choose presence over performance in your heart, your actions, and your home? Be specific. This is the only way you will truly change.

Pray: Talk with God about the motives of your heart. Ask that he will help you discover more hope every day as you choose presence over performance with him and others.

Day 4: Rediscovering Community

Read: Matthew 18:19–20; Colossians 3:9–16; Philippians 2:1–4

During my darkest days of recovery and restoration, God sent friends who were willing to surround me with love. These men are my closest friends to this day—including my pastor and a whole crew of people I consider my extended family. They were my sounding board during the impossible days and my guides during the darkest ones.

But they were also the same men whom I had lied to repeatedly and kept at arms-length when I was in denial and living my own way instead of God's way. I was known as the guy who was *unashamed*, so I wasn't about to admit to my closest friends just how *ashamed* I actually felt about my actions, my thoughts, and my words. It was easier just to push everyone away instead of owning up to the reality of the chaos in my life. I rationalized my addictive behaviors by comparing myself to people who I thought were worse off than me. But I discovered that whenever you say something in your life is not "that bad," and you're hiding it from your family and your closest friends, you're on the path to self-destruction.

At that point, I knew I had to have hard conversations with the friends in my life whom I had spent years evading. I met with these men and came clean about how I was avoiding them and working around the accountability structures they helped me put in place years earlier. I had to own up to the partial truths I had been telling them. And I confessed that I really just wanted them to be my "yes men" for a season. The truth is, they had been seeing everything I had been doing all along and still loved me. When I came clean, they showered me with grace and mercy I hadn't realized was possible. I was rediscovering community with these men and, in doing so, I was also rediscovering God through them.

What does Jesus mean when he says, "Where two or three are gathered in my name, there I am with them" (Matthew 18:20)? How have you experienced the power of God in community with others?

Which people in your community reflect the love, mercy, and grace of God to you? Explain.

What encouragements and instructions did Paul give to the Colossians on how to interact with each other? Just like Paul in his encouragement to the Philippians, how are you looking out for the interests of others—and not just your own?

How have you had to ask for forgiveness or offer forgiveness to a friend? What was this like for you? What did you learn from that experience?

Pray: Talk with God about the way you show up in your community. Ask that he will bring you a community of friends who bring out the best in you as you seek to love him and love others.

Day 5: Failure and Forgiveness

Read: Philippians 4:10–13; 1 Corinthians 4:1–5; 1 Corinthians 9:24–27; Ephesians 2:1–10

When I finally came face to face with my own self-righteousness and realized I had lived this way for most of my life, I was able to accept my failures and the forgiveness I needed in those failures. This was a hard thing for me to do, because I had spent so much time and energy being self-righteous with everyone around me, keeping score when they faltered or failed. But never once did I pause to take a long hard look at my own failures.

Here's why I think this is an issue for more people than just me. In American churches today, we love referencing and speaking about the apostle Paul. We hone on things he said as if he was almost Christlike. But if you ask me, I think we've turned this into an overemphasis on constructing a Pauline-dependent faith rather than a Christ-centered faith. Paul was human. He was an apostle with faults just like the rest of us. He was following the standard set by Jesus and recognizing that he himself was not the standard.

This is why Paul wrote about not wanting to be disqualified from the prize due to his preaching. Paul was sure of the gospel message of Jesus, but not always sure of himself as the message bearer. That's why he talked about passing judgment on himself and God being his judge. Paul was declaring that he didn't have what it takes to be capable on his own. But he could still preach the power of the gospel because it was the power of God, not his own power.

For Paul, God was the source of every good thing. And yet somehow we have a tendency to twist Paul's perspective and read him through the lens of self-righteousness and self-sufficiency. We tell ourselves that if Paul had the power to "do all things" through Christ, then we have the power to keep pushing through as well. We emphasize Paul and lose sight of the source of Paul's ability to keep pressing on: Christ. We miss that Paul is saying he can do all things *through* Christ. Paul was being self-deprecating, not self-righteous.

When I started to see Paul in this way, I could put myself in his place and own up to my own failures. But I needed grace to deal with the shame and guilt of acknowledging my failures. Guilt told me, *You've failed!* Shame told me, *You're a failure!* But Jesus reminded me, *Your failures are forgiven.* Seeing Paul in a new light changed everything for me.

After considering the idea of Paul as a self-deprecating human rather than a self-righteous Christlike figure, what stands out to you about Paul's posture in these passages?

What exactly is Paul doing through the strength of Christ in his letter to the Ephesians? What are you doing through the strength of Christ in your life?

How have you been self-righteous and judgmental of others? What failures and faults do you need to stop ignoring and start acknowledging?

Paul says it is by grace we have been saved through faith, and this grace is a gift from God. In what ways does accepting God's gift of grace and forgiveness change the way you live your life?

Pray: Talk with God about the forgiveness he gives in spite of your failures. Lean on his grace to move beyond the guilt and shame of those failures and do the work he has prepared for you.

For Next Week

Use the space below to write any insights or questions that you want to discuss at the next group meeting. In preparation for next week, read chapters 8–9 in I Am Restored.

Walking in the Light

I am making everything new!

REVELATION 21:5

Welcome

I found something new in this difficult season of my life. Yes, I went through hell, but the fire forged a new me. I realized God was making a masterpiece out of my mess. It was an unfinished masterpiece, but that's because God was inviting me to help him make the masterpiece of my life *together*. I had a part to play—a role in my own agency. But this required me to follow Jesus in light of his love and grace without trying to prove myself to him.

In my early years, I tried so hard to reach theological perfection. But this only exhausted my soul. It only led to the flipside of someone else proving me wrong; and being wrong terrified me more than being broken. The cycle heaped shame and guilt on top of my depression and anxiety. But as I got healthy, I began to realize that shame and guilt could no longer be motivators. I was God's masterpiece, not someone else's, or even my own. I didn't need the approval or affirmation of others the way I did prior to this season in my life. God was helping me write a new story—a story of light and love anchored in his hope and promise of healing.

After my last-ditch effort to find my faith on the trip to Egypt, I knew I needed to actively participate in my own healing. So, I put my life on pause for a few months. Just like my professional athlete friends, I would have to address my injury—clinical depression—and wait for it to heal while doing the hard work of rehab. Acting as though the injury or problem didn't exist was easier, but my marriage, my family, my friendships, and my faith hinged on whether I was willing to do the hard work of healing.

The hardest part was *actively pursuing* health. I had to be honest about how unhealthy my mind truly was. I had to fully accept my identity in God—that I was truly loved, truly accepted, truly known, and had nothing to prove. I spent time just sitting still in the presence of God instead of proving that I had the right head knowledge about God.

The more I slowed down, the more I began to heal. Therapy, reading God's Word, rhythms, and rituals with my family all became part of the regular reset required to keep away the dysfunction and chaos. I became more of a human *being*, less of a human *doing*. A healthy lifestyle is what allowed me to keep walking in God's light. The same will be true for you as well.

Share

Begin your group time by inviting those in the group to share their insights from last week's personal study. Then, to kick things off, discuss one of the following questions:

- What comes to mind when you consider your life as God's masterpiece?

—*or*—

- What is easier for you—to be a human *being* or a human *doing*?

Read

Invite someone to read aloud Psalm 56:1–13. Listen for fresh insights as you hear the verses being read, and then discuss the questions that follow.

> ¹ Be merciful to me, my God,
>> for my enemies are in hot pursuit;
>> all day long they press their attack.
> ² My adversaries pursue me all day long;
>> in their pride many are attacking me.
> ³ When I am afraid, I put my trust in you.
>> ⁴ In God, whose word I praise—
> in God I trust and am not afraid.
>> What can mere mortals do to me?
> ⁵ All day long they twist my words;
>> all their schemes are for my ruin.
> ⁶ They conspire, they lurk,
>> they watch my steps,
>> hoping to take my life.
> ⁷ Because of their wickedness do not let them escape;
>> in your anger, God, bring the nations down.
> ⁸ Record my misery;

list my tears on your scroll—
are they not in your record?
9 Then my enemies will turn back
when I call for help.
By this I will know that God is for me.
10 In God, whose word I praise,
in the LORD, whose word I praise—
11 in God I trust and am not afraid.
What can man do to me?
12 I am under vows to you, my God;
I will present my thank offerings to you.
13 For you have delivered me from death
and my feet from stumbling,
that I may walk before God
in the light of life.

What do you notice about David's pursuit of God in this passage?

What did David determine to do in spite of what he was feeling?

The Context

David had many enemies: King Saul, Doeg the Edomite, the Philistines, those from his own household, and others. A superscript included in the text of this psalm indicates that David composed it while hiding out from Saul in the Philistine city of Gath. According to the story told in 1 Samuel 21:10–15, David was captured by Achish, the king of the city, and ultimately feigned madness so the Philistines would not view him as a threat and let him go. David evidently wrote the psalm while imprisoned and waiting to learn his fate. It was a dark time—one of many such dark periods in his life—and he was afraid and uncertain about his future. Yet in the middle of his darkness and doubt, he could still turn to God as his source of light. As a result, David has gone down in history as being "a man after [God's] own heart" (Acts 13:22).

Watch

Play the video segment for session four (see the streaming video access provided on the inside front cover). As you watch, use the following outline to record any thoughts or concepts that stand out to you.

Taking a step back to pursue healing

Finding peace

Drifting on the undercurrent of disconnection

The missed opportunities

Owning the darkness . . . by starting therapy

Self-care is taking care of our God-given mind, body, and soul

Practicing healthy perspectives on the journey toward restoration:

- Weekly sabbath

- Meditating on God's Word

- Seeing our story in God's bigger story

- Being aware that God restores through hope and healing

Restoration is an ongoing process, not a one-time event

We can journey toward restoration—toward the life God initially created for us

Character Study

If David could walk through dark times of impending death, imprisonment, and an uncertain future, and yet still go down in history as "a man after God's own heart" (Acts 13:22), then the same can be true for us. Our life circumstances may be very different from David's, but we can still find ourselves in the story of David as the bold young shepherd (see 1 Samuel 16), the brave warrior (see 1 Samuel 17), the hunted (see 1 Samuel 19), the best friend (see 1 Samuel 20), and certainly the sinner (see 2 Samuel 11). The ups and downs of David's life are proof that we can be men and women after God's own heart even if we've experienced chaos, turmoil, and doubt about God in our own lives.

Imagine what could also be said about our lives if we recognize that it is *never too late to turn to God as our source of light.* This is what David did, and what the apostle Paul and other faith-filled people throughout the centuries have done. Their example serves as a guide to us. We don't have to wait for a crisis to turn to God for restoration, hope, and healing. We can learn from these stories of others to see God as a source of light, no matter our situation.

God doesn't promise to always clear the chaos from our lives, but he does promise to always be with us (see Deuteronomy 31:6). David reminds us that God is also our help in times of trouble (see Psalm 46:1). As was true for David, God's presence gives us hope in our journey of healing and restoration.

Discuss

Take a few minutes with your group members to discuss what you just watched and explore these concepts in Scripture.

1. What stood out to you from listening to Lecrae today? In what ways have you been drifting away from connection with God and with those close to you?

2. As Lecrae mentioned during the teaching, sometimes the best thing we can do in the middle of the chaos is take a break. Taking a break can look like a sabbatical, a vacation, or even a walk outside around the block. How do you think taking a break would help you? In what ways does taking a break help you see things from a different perspective?

3. Lecrae notes that he found the courage to walk toward the hope and healing of restoration when he reconnected with God. As Jesus said to his disciples, "Remain in me, as I also remain in you. No branch can bear fruit by itself; it must remain in the vine. Neither can you bear fruit unless you remain in me" (John 15:4). What are the benefits of remaining in Jesus, especially during difficult seasons?

4. When we actively pursue healing in God, we find that it frames our current struggles in a different light. We come to know that God is with us and working for us in the midst of the trial. David came to this realization. In the midst of fleeing for his life, he could still write, "I sought the LORD, and he answered me; he delivered me from all my fears. Those who look to him are radiant; their faces are never covered with shame" (Psalm 34:4–5). How has your perspective on your trials changed as you have sought God?

5. **Read 1 John 1:5–7.** What choices are you making to walk in God's light? What will you start doing or stop doing today to stay in his light?

6. Lecrae speaks in this session of the life-changing truth of how God makes all things new. As you look back over the last few sessions of discovering the truth about your own story by hearing the restoration story of Lecrae, how is God making you new?

Respond

Briefly review the outline for the video teaching and any notes you took. In the space below, write down the most significant point you took away from this session.

Pray

Pray as a group before you close your time together. Thank God for the way he illuminates your path toward healing and restoration. Ask him to provide the perseverance required to continually travel the road to rehabilitation and to increasingly bring godly friends into your life who will help you along the way. Pray that you will see the masterpiece he is creating you to be.

SESSION FOUR

Final Personal Study

Reflect on the material you covered during this week's group time by engaging in the following personal studies. Each day offers a short reading adapted from I Am Restored, along with a few reflection questions to take you deeper into the theme of this week's study. Be sure to read the reflection questions and make a few notes in your guide about the experience. In the coming days, take a few minutes to share any insights that you learned with one of your fellow group members.

Day One: Drifting Away

Read: Mark 4:35–41; Hebrews 2:1–4; Hebrews 6:13–20

I remember a trip I took to the Pacific Ocean with my daughter and her friend. We arrived at the beach, just two dads and their two daughters, and the girls were so excited to jump in the water. Of course, I had a list of instructions for them: *no talking to strangers, no wandering outside my sight, no hanging with kids who weren't part of our group, and don't go out in the water too far.* The last instruction was the most important because of the undercurrent that could take them out into the ocean beyond the reach of help.

I watched while the girls played in the water for a while. And while they never floated out too deep into the ocean, they began to drift laterally—off to the side. The shift wasn't dramatic, but slowly and subtly they drifted farther and farther down the beach, away from my watchful eyes. The undercurrent wasn't carrying them out, but it was still carrying them away.

This is such a great metaphor for what happens when we don't address the issues in our lives. We slowly drift far away from the place we were intended and created to be. The shift is slow and subtle. We don't see it immediately, but then one day we look up in shock and realize how far we've landed from where we wanted to go. The waves of chaos will carry us away to self-destruction if we're not careful. If we want to live healthy lives according to God's plan, we have to adjust our ways of thinking and living to find where we're supposed to be.

When I realized how far I had drifted from the healthy place that God intended me to be, I felt broken. But ironically, for the first time, I wasn't embarrassed to be broken. I truly felt like God took joy in me and was pulling me back to the place he wanted me to be. He met me on my way back to him. It was as though he "swam out to meet me" as I battled the undercurrent of my past pain and the chaos of my choices. I was now safe in the presence of God. And beyond my rekindled relationship with God, I was overwhelmed by how deeply my community loved me. They were still there for me even though I had drifted away from them as well.

How have you experienced this slow drift toward unhealthy choices and patterns? What specific circumstances or situations have made you feel like you are drowning?

How do you want Jesus to calm the storm of your life? Do you have faith he can do it?

The author of Hebrews says that we must "pay the most careful attention . . . to what we have heard, so that we do not drift away" (Hebrews 2:1). What does the author mean by this statement? What are we to remember about "what we have heard"?

What does it mean to have "hope as an anchor for the soul" (Hebrews 6:19)?

Pray: Talk with God about the healthy place that he intends for you to be today. Ask that he will lead you back to that place no matter how far you may have drifted away.

Day Two: No Big Deal

Read: John 9:1–34; Luke 18:35–43; John 5:1–15

This season of my life was slowly shaping me into something new. The problem was I didn't even know what "new" should or could look like because of the blinding nature of my pain. I only knew I had to acknowledge the pain and move forward. I had learned the hard way that if I was too attached to who I was, I would always be afraid to be the person God called me to be.

The key to my healing was fully embracing who I was supposed to be as a man and as a human being created in God's image. The amount of work I faced in counseling almost drowned me, but the exertion eventually led to healing. But in order to get there, I had to abolish a particular phrase I had used way too often: "It's *no big deal.*" I frequently used this phrase when referring to my past as a way to numb the pain. I was a kid without a father . . . *no big deal.* I was abused as a child . . . *no big deal.* My emotions had been minimized by caregivers . . . *no big deal.* I was forced into violent situations by men who thought I was a mama's boy . . . *no big deal.* I was spiritually abused by people in power in the church I called my home . . . *no big deal.* I was slammed on social media by people who didn't like my perspective . . . *no big deal.* I was called a "mascot" and a "sellout" by my fellow black Christian peers . . . *no big deal.*

If I said it was *no big deal*, then it couldn't hurt me. *They* couldn't hurt me. Or so I thought. I had to start acknowledging the trauma and wounds that I had referred to as *no big deal.* It was a time for breaking and pruning. And one of the things I had to prune was this phrase. Abuse, trauma, and wounds—no matter how big or small—*are a big deal.* Even when our minds convince us otherwise, our body still keeps the score of these experiences. We have to stop minimizing our pain if we're going to find healing and restoration. The only way out of the darkness is to go *through* it all until we can see the light at the end of the tunnel.

Healing is a big deal. The story that John relates of Jesus healing the man born blind is actually a story of two types of blindness. Jesus healed the man of physical *blindness. But the Pharisees' reaction indicates that they suffered from* spiritual *blindness. How does spiritual blindness keep us from "seeing" our wounds and keep us from the healing that needs to take place?*

What do you notice about the way the crowd responded to the blind man near Jericho in the story told in Luke? What do you notice about the way Jesus responded to the man?

Jesus asked the lame man by the Pool of Bethesda a crucial question we all need to consider: Do you want to get well? Think about your answer and write down your honest thoughts here.

Is there a phrase you've used to minimize the pain of your past? Write it down here. What would you need to do to stop using this phrase in your life?

Pray: Talk with God about the ways you have minimized your pain, the way your pain has been minimized by others, and even the way you may have minimized someone else's pain. Ask God to help you "see the light at the end of the tunnel" and provide you with his hope.

Day Three: Rhythm over Routine

Read: Matthew 14:1–36; Mark 3:1–12; John 7:14–24

It was a lot harder for me to take an extended sabbatical to rest and recover than to just keep working and trying to figure out my problems along the way. But it was *necessary.* And it was something Jesus modeled so well. Multiple times in Scripture, we read how he stepped away from the crowds to spend time with God and be with his Father.

By regularly taking a break from his ministry schedule, Jesus was modeling mental health for us. He was showing us that slipping away from all the noise is necessary at times to preserve our sanity. By healing people on the Sabbath, Jesus was also breaking away from the rules and the routine of the Torah. In doing so, he was showing us that we can maintain a Sabbath rhythm even when we break from routine.

Truth is, the routine of life can wear down our souls and destroy our ability to be present in the moment. Over time, we start to serve our routines instead of our routines serving and benefiting us. When this happens, we tend to choose productivity and efficiency over health and rest. But what's healthy for us should always take precedence.

If I wanted to continue to heal from my depression, I knew I had to engage my heart, soul, body, and mind in new rhythms, so I didn't fall back into the dysfunctional patterns of my own routines. Modeled by the life of Jesus, I knew I needed a rhythm of *daily distractions, weekly withdrawals,* and *annual abandonments.* I replaced my daily distractions of social media consumption with meditation, time being fully present with my wife and kids, reading God's Word, and physical exercise. My weekly withdrawals now included therapy with a mental health counselor and a true sabbath day of rest. And my annual abandonment now looked like taking a vacation with my wife regardless of my tour schedule or music career.

I knew I could either willingly unplug from my life for a time or be forced to take a permanent vacation by making wrong choices to destroy my life. So I started studying the ancient rhythms of sabbath-keeping to keep me mindful of the choices I made every day, each week, and every year to pause, rest, enjoy God's creation, and remind myself that I was not in control. I am convinced that healthy rhythms allow us to actively pursue healthy and whole lives. This is what brings us joy.

In the stories told in Matthew, Jesus withdrew to a solitary place not just once, but twice. What do you learn from Jesus about pulling away even in the midst of a crowd or a full season of life?

In the story told in Mark, why were the Pharisees okay with circumcision but not healing on the Sabbath? How was Jesus "making things new" for the first-century religious leaders and Jews?

In the story told in John, how did the Pharisees react to Jesus? What does this tell you about the way you might be judged as you pursue God's course for your life?

What does it look like for you to prioritize rest and health in your life? Where do you need to break from routine and begin a new rhythm?

Pray: Talk with God about the pattern of your life. Ask him to help you find rest and healing in new rhythms of life as you break from the past dysfunction of unhealthy routines.

Day Four: Finding Our Way Back Home

Read: Genesis 1:26–31; Psalm 139:1–24; 2 Corinthians 5:16–21

We all love watching athletes of the highest level dazzle us with their ability on the field or the court. They give everything they have to the game, and many of them are fortunate enough to make millions of dollars and attract a ton of attention. But for some athletes, celebrities included, that kind of fame and attention not only drenches them in the spotlight—it eventually drowns them. Ultimately, every action is micro-analyzed and critiqued by millions of people.

While celebrities and athletes are easy targets for us to analyze, what about everyday people? The stress of performing for everyone else, impressing our relational partners, or working to receive recognition can (and will) drown most of us if we're not careful. When our identity is so bound up with other people, we don't know how to be a healthy version of ourselves on our own. We start asking ourselves questions like, *Who am I?* and *What do I have to offer the world outside of this role?* We long to be known for who we are, not for what we do. We long to find our way home—our way back to a true sense of self we have when we are rooted in the image of God. But it's our false sense of self that is often appealing to the fleeting praise of people, even when that false sense of self is wounded and broken.

Navigating our way out of a *false* sense of self and finding our way back home to a *true* sense of self requires change—and change is hard. When some people reach this point, they decide not to risk it, because change requires removing part of them that they once associated with a core identity. It's the reason professional athletes and celebrities struggle after retiring from the spotlight.

But we either take the painful risk to change the core of our identity by finding our way back to our true sense of self or we drown in our own dysfunction.

When I was at this crossroad in my own journey, I was working to achieve, to be approved of, to find acceptance from God and from others. Finding my way back home to God meant finding my way back home to my identity in God, back to the *real me*. And when I could see the real God in the real me, I knew I was where I belonged.

How would you describe the difference between your false sense of self (who you are based on what others expect) and your true sense of self (who you are as an image-bearer of God)?

What stands out to you about David's discovery in Psalm 139 of his true sense of self in God?

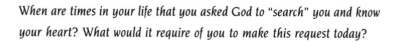

When are times in your life that you asked God to "search" you and know your heart? What would it require of you to make this request today?

Paul writes, "If anyone is in Christ, the new creation has come: The old has gone, the new is here!" (2 Corinthians 5:17). What does it mean to be a new creation in Christ? How does this involve putting aside the false self and embracing the true self?

Pray: Talk with God about your search for your identity—your true sense of self—found in Christ. Ask him to help you make the changes necessary for you to embrace your true identity.

Day Five: Working Together for Our Good

Read: Romans 8:22–39; 2 Corinthians 12:6–10; Psalm 28:6–9

In many churches today, mental health has been separated from theology. Many don't believe they need a counselor if they have a relationship with Jesus. But there is no conflict between mental health and spiritual health. In fact, it's quite the opposite—they're interconnected.

I firmly believe we need to use *all* the gifts God has given us, including the expertise of those who are qualified and equipped to walk with people through mental darkness. Note that I say *qualified*—too many counseling services offered today are from those who are not professionally licensed or trained. Just because someone gives good advice does not mean they are a mental health therapist. No shortcuts or over-spiritualized clichés will work here.

In my own life, mental health counseling became a necessary means of self-correction. It was part of my self-care, and it was about addressing my whole self from a holistic perspective. If my mind was not healthy, it would hinder me from functioning as a healthy human being overall. This is why mental health requires self-awareness—the willingness to see destructive patterns and ask for guidance to break those patterns and learn what healthy living can truly be. Self-care, including mental health counseling, has allowed for a regular reset in my life from the areas of dysfunction into which I have a tendency to drift.

Of course, therapy was not without its challenges. I wanted someone who could see me as the black man, the believer, and the artist I was, and respect all of these parts of me. And truthfully, it took a few months before I found the right counselor. After I did, therapy became a safe place for me to acknowledge and process my trauma. Had I denied this experience because of the shame I felt from pursuing mental health, I would not be *restored* the way I am today.

I needed theology *and* therapy. And my guess is, someday you will too.

How has your perspective of therapy been shaped by your theology? And how has your perspective been encouraged or challenged by Lecrae's message?

What do you think Paul meant when he wrote that "God works for the good of those who love him, who have been called according to his purpose" (Romans 8:28)?

How can you relate to Paul's plea in 2 Corinthians 12:8 to God to remove his "thorn"?

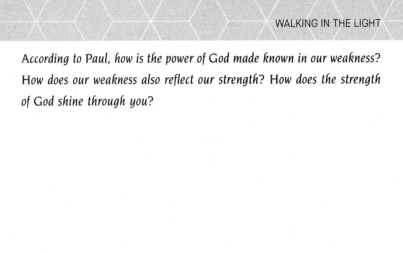

According to Paul, how is the power of God made known in our weakness? How does our weakness also reflect our strength? How does the strength of God shine through you?

What hope do you gain from David's words in Psalm 28 that God is always working for your good? In what area of your life do you need his strength today?

Pray: Talk with God about the way he is working all things together for your good. Ask him to help you lean into his strength as you continue your journey to pursue healing and restoration.

Leader's Guide

Thank you for your willingness to lead your group through this study. What you have chosen to do is valuable and will make a great difference in the lives of others. The rewards of being a leader are different from those of participating, and we hope that as you lead you will find your own walk with Jesus deepened by the experience.

I Am Restored is a four-session Bible study built around video content and small-group interaction. As the group leader, imagine yourself as the host of a dinner party. Your job is to take care of your guests by managing the behind-the-scenes details so that as your guests arrive, they can focus on one another and on the interaction around the topic for that week.

As the group leader, your role is not to answer all the questions or reteach the content—the video, book, and study guide will do most of that work. Your job is to guide the experience and cultivate your small group into a connected and engaged community. This will make it a place for members to process, question, and reflect—not receive more instruction.

There are several elements in this leader's guide that will help you as you structure your study and reflection time, so be sure to follow along and take advantage of each one.

Before You Begin

Before your first meeting, make sure the group members have a copy of this study guide. Alternately, you can hand out the study guides at your first meeting and give the group members some time to look over the material and ask any preliminary questions. Also make sure they are aware that they have access to the videos at any time through the streaming code provided on the inside front cover. During your first meeting, send a sheet of paper around the room and have the members write down their name, phone number, and email address so you can keep in touch with them during the week.

Generally, the ideal size for a group is eight to ten people, which will ensure that everyone has enough time to participate in discussions. If you have more people, you might want to break up the main group into smaller subgroups. Encourage those who show up at the first meeting to commit to attending the duration of the study, as this will help the group members get to know one another, create stability for the group, and help you as the leader know how to best prepare each week.

Each of the sessions begins with an opening reflection. The questions that follow in the "Share" section serve as an icebreaker to get the group members thinking about the general topic at hand. Some people may want to tell a long story in response to one of these questions, but the goal is to keep the answers brief. Ideally, you want everyone in the group to get a chance to answer, so try to keep the responses to a minute or less. If you have talkative group members, say up front that everyone needs to limit their answer to one minute.

Give the group members a chance to answer, but tell them to feel free to pass if they wish. With the rest of the study, it's generally not a good idea to have everyone answer every question—a free-flowing discussion is more desirable. But with the opening icebreaker-type questions, you can go around the circle. Encourage shy people to share, but don't force them.

At your first meeting, let the group members know each session contains a personal study section that they can use to reflect more on the content during the week. While this is an optional exercise, it will help the members cement the concepts presented during the group study time and encourage them to spend time each day in God's Word. Let them know that if they choose to do so, they can watch the video for the following week by accessing the streaming code found on the inside front cover of their studies. Invite them to bring any questions and insights they uncovered while reading to your next meeting, especially if they had a breakthrough moment or didn't understand something.

Weekly Preparation

As the leader, there are a few things you should do to prepare for each meeting:

- *Read through the session.* This will help you to become more familiar with the content and know how to structure the discussion times.
- *Decide how the videos will be used.* Determine whether you want the members to watch the videos ahead of time (via the streaming access code found on the inside front cover) or together as a group.
- *Decide which questions you want to discuss.* Based on the amount and length of group discussion, you may not be able to get

through all the questions, so choose four to five that you definitely want to cover.

- Be *familiar with the questions you want to discuss.* When the group meets, you'll be watching the clock, so you want to make sure you are familiar with the questions you have selected. In this way, you'll ensure you have the material more deeply in your mind than your group members.
- *Pray for your group.* Pray for your group members throughout the week and ask God to lead them as they study his Word.

In many cases, there will be no one "right" answer to the question. Answers will vary, especially when the group members are being asked to share their personal experiences.

Structuring the Discussion Time

You will need to determine with your group how long you want to meet each week so you can plan your time accordingly. Generally, most groups like to meet for either ninety minutes or two hours, so you could use one of the following schedules:

Section	90 Minutes	120 Minutes
WELCOME (members arrive and get settled)	10 minutes	15 minutes
SHARE (discuss one or more of the opening questions for the session)	15 minutes	20 minutes
WATCH (watch the teaching material together and take notes)	25 minutes	25 minutes
DISCUSS (discuss the Bible study questions you selected ahead of time)	30 minutes	45 minutes
RESPOND / PRAY (reflect on the message, pray together as a group, and dismiss)	10 minutes	15 minutes

As the group leader, it is up to you to keep track of the time and keep things on schedule. You might want to set a timer for each segment so both you and the group members know when your time is up. (There are some good phone apps for timers that play a gentle chime or other pleasant sound instead of a disruptive noise.)

Don't be concerned if the group members are quiet or slow to share. People are often quiet when they are pulling together their ideas, and this might be a new experience for them. Just ask a question and let it hang in the air until someone shares. You can then say, "Thank you. What about others? What came to you when you watched that portion of the teaching?"

Group Dynamics

Leading a group through I Am Restored will prove to be highly rewarding both to you and your group members. But you still may encounter challenges along the way! Discussions can get off track. Group members may not be sensitive to the needs and ideas of others. Some might worry they will be expected to talk about matters that make them feel awkward. Others may express comments that result in disagreements. To help ease this strain on you and the group, consider the following ground rules:

- When someone raises a question or comment that is off the main topic, suggest that you deal with it another time, or, if you feel led to go in that direction, let the group know you will be spending some time discussing it.
- If someone asks a question that you don't know how to answer, admit it and move on. At your discretion, feel free

to invite group members to comment on questions that call for personal experience.

- If you find one or two people are dominating the discussion time, direct a few questions to others in the group. Outside the main group time, ask the more dominating members to help you draw out the quieter ones. Work to make them a part of the solution instead of part of the problem.

- When a disagreement occurs, encourage the group members to process the matter in love. Encourage those on opposite sides to restate what they heard the other side say about the matter, and then invite each side to evaluate if that perception is accurate. Lead the group in examining other Scriptures related to the topic and look for common ground.

When any of these issues arise, encourage your group members to follow these words from the Bible: "Love one another" (John 13:34), "If it is possible, as far as it depends on you, live at peace with everyone" (Romans 12:18), "Whatever is true . . . noble . . . right . . . if anything is excellent or praiseworthy—think about such things" (Philippians 4:8), and "Be quick to listen, slow to speak and slow to become angry" (James 1:19). This will make your group time more rewarding and beneficial for everyone who attends.

Thank you again for your willingness to lead your group. May God reward your efforts and dedication, equip you to guide your group in the weeks ahead, and make your time together in I Am Restored fruitful as you pursue God's health and wholeness.

ALSO AVAILABLE

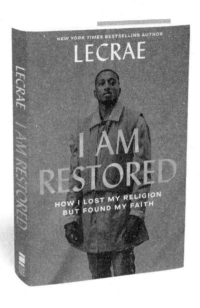

The untold story of how Lecrae's past nearly ruined his life—until he learned that the wounds we carry point to the healing and freedom we all desperately need.

When all you've suffered threatens to destroy your life, how do you get back to the truth you thought you believed?

"This personal story of faith lost and found is especially recommended to Christians who are struggling to comprehend God's complex ways."

—LIBRARY JOURNAL

"If you want to understand how to transform your life experiences into a personal catalyst for your growth, look no further."

—KIRK FRANKLIN

"Grammy Award–winning hip-hop artist Lecrae delves into his struggles, shame, and destructive habits in this powerful follow-up to his 2016 memoir *Unashamed....* Lecrae's fans will love this."

—PUBLISHERS WEEKLY

"This book helps us. It has helped me. Write on, Lecrae. Your words are healing us."

—PRISCILLA SHIRER, Bible teacher and *New York Times* bestselling author

Available in stores and online!